Not For The Fainthearted

The Ultimate Challenge For Men

Tinashe Munyaradzi

authorHOUSE®

AuthorHouse™
1663 Liberty Drive
Bloomington, IN 47403
www.authorhouse.com
Phone: 1-800-839-8640

First published by AuthorHouse   5/14/2009

ISBN: 978-1-4389-8624-1 (e)
ISBN: 978-1-4389-8623-4 (sc)
ISBN: 978-1-4389-8622-7 (hc)

Printed in the United States of America
Bloomington, Indiana

This book is printed on acid-free paper.

Unless otherwise noted, all Scriptures are taken from the Holy Bible.
New Living Translation copyright © 1996, 2004

Dedication

To the greatest woman I have ever known,
to the most energetic woman who is my motivator,
to the most generous woman who has ceaselessly offered support
for me and the call of God on my life,
I lovingly dedicate this book to you, Bester.
You are indeed better than Best.
I also dedicate this book to our two beautiful daughters, Anesu
and Tivonge. May the Lord clothe you with all the virtues that
constitute women of God.

Acknowledgments

I am sincerely grateful to all those from whom I have learned valuable lessons that have contributed to make me the man I am.

I would like to express my appreciation to my family, whose all-encompassing support and patience was a tremendous blessing, especially during the time of writing this book.

To the members of Dallas International Fellowship and to all our friends and family —thank you for your prayers and encouragement.

I am thankful also to Pastor Arvel Wilson and the men at West Dallas Community Church. You all inspired me by your passion for truth.

Apostle George Chikohwa, I thank you for challenging me and setting me up to write this book.

I deeply thank the Lord and you for the privilege of sharing these life-changing truths.

Contents

Prologue

In order for you to have maximum benefit from this book, we need to be in agreement about the following three points:

1. Everything that you know right now you have learned from someone.

2. What you have learned so far is not everything there is to know.

3. Some of the things that you know are not true.

With these three points in mind, I ask you as you read through this book to be patient. Please be patient with me, be patient with yourself, and be patient with God.

Introduction

In the Bible, there is a very fascinating instruction that God gave to His people, the Israelites. This instruction is recorded in the book of Deuteronomy, chapter 20, verse 8. The Israelites had to observe this order whenever they went to battle against their enemies.

This is what is written: *"Then the officers shall speak further to the people and say, 'Who is the man that is afraid and fainthearted? Let him depart and return to his house, so that he might not make his brothers' hearts melt like his heart.'"*

What is interesting to note is that whenever the officers of the Israeli army would make this announcement, many men actually returned to their houses. In at least one occasion, twenty-two thousand out of thirty-two thousand men went back home from the battlefront! This particular account is recorded in the book called Judges in chapter 7 from verse 1 to verse 3.

Here is the implicit statement made by these fainthearted men: "We would rather go home, and let the enemy subjugate us and our people than to be strong and go fight!" I can hear you say, "What cowardice!" Yes, spinelessness indeed! Especially when you discover that the enemy that the twenty-two thousand men had qualms fighting against was later defeated by an army of only three hundred men!

From this account, it is clear that the magnitude of the external odds that a man is up against has nothing to do with faintheartedness. The kind of spirit that resides in a man's bosom is what gives rise to either fear or faith. The kind of spirit that was in the three hundred men enabled them to believe that they could defeat their enemies—even though the enemies were much greater in number than them.

As we fight on to rescue marriages, families, and communities, the odds against us are meaningless. The statistics are insignificant. There is a desperate need for men who have the courage to look at truth, embrace it, and appropriate it to their daily lives. A fainthearted man would rather die than change!

You may be a perfect gentleman who does not want to talk about gruesome things. Maybe you are opposed to war. I am sorry to be the one to tell you that, by virtue of being alive, you are involved in warfare! You may not believe this, but you don't have to. Life is a battle. Even if you don't want to fight, you will be fought against. It is dangerous to have all kinds of bullets and missiles flying all around you and you not know what is going on.

As you read this book with rapt attention, here is the issue that you will need to resolve, hopefully sooner than later: Are you now going to muster the courage to fight the battle of life with intentionality, or are you going to opt to return "home" to your comfort zone? Are you going to turn back to your stubborn pride, excuses, and indifference instead of fighting the lies that have been unleashed with full force against humanity?

Chapter 1

If You Met Yourself, Would You Be Able To Recognize Yourself?

It is well for people who think to change their minds occasionally in order to keep them clean.—Luther Burbank

There is a very well-known king in the Bible named David. One time the prophet went to the king and wittingly told David a story about David! The prophet effectively placed a mirror right in front of the king. Amusingly, David looked so deplorable that David failed to recognize himself! The prophet had to introduce David to David! This is a disease that many men have. They fail to see themselves in the women around them. Here is the story as it is found in 2 Samuel 12 from verse 1.

> **Many men fail to see themselves in the women around them.**

¹ *So the* LORD *sent Nathan the prophet to tell David this story: "There were two men in a certain town. One was rich, and one was poor.*

² *The rich man owned a great many sheep and cattle.*

³ *The poor man owned nothing but one little lamb he had bought. He raised that little lamb, and it grew up with his children. It ate from the man's own plate and drank from his cup. He cuddled it in his arms like a baby daughter.*

⁴ *One day a guest arrived at the home of the rich man. But instead of killing an animal from his own flock or herd, he took the poor man's lamb and killed it and prepared it for his guest."*

⁵ *David was furious. "As surely as the* LORD *lives," he vowed, "any man who would do such a thing deserves to die!*

⁶ *He must repay four lambs to the poor man for the one he stole and for having no pity."*

⁷ *Then Nathan said to David,* "**You are that man***!* [Emphasis added]

The LORD*, the God of Israel, says: I anointed you king of Israel and saved you from the power of Saul.*

⁸ *I gave you your master's house and his wives and the kingdoms of Israel and Judah. And if that had not been enough, I would have given you much, much more.*

⁹ *Why, then, have you despised the word of the* LORD *and done this horrible deed? For you have murdered Uriah the Hittite with the sword of the Ammonites and stolen his wife.*

¹⁰ From this time on, your family will live by the sword because you have despised me by taking Uriah's wife to be your own."

David, who already had several wives, had orchestrated the killing of one of his military commanders named Uriah in order to take Uriah's wife!

Before getting too hard on David, it is only fair to highlight the fact that David's own great-great-great-granddaddy had previously acted the same way as David acted in this account. This great ancestor of David was named Judah. For Judah's story, let us refer again to the Bible. Here is what is written in the book of Genesis in chapter 38 starting from verse 12:

¹² Some years later Judah's wife died. After the time of mourning was over, Judah and his friend Hirah the Adullamite went up to Timnah to supervise the shearing of his sheep.
¹³ Someone told Tamar, "Look, your father-in-law is going up to Timnah to shear his sheep."

Tamar was Judah's daughter-in-law, whom Judah had sent back to her parents. This happened after Tamar's second husband had died. Judah sent Tamar away with a promise that when Judah's third son, Shelah, became of marriageable age, Judah would arrange the marriage between Tamar and Shelah. This was in keeping with the traditions of Judah's culture.

¹⁴ Tamar was aware that Shelah had grown up, but no arrangements had been made for her to come and marry him. So she changed out of her widow's clothing and covered herself with a veil to disguise herself. Then she sat beside the road at the entrance to the village of Enaim, which is on the road to Timnah.

¹⁵ *Judah noticed her and thought she was a prostitute, since she had covered her face.*

¹⁶ *So he stopped and propositioned her. "Let me have sex with you," he said, not realizing that she was his own daughter-in-law.*

"How much will you pay to have sex with me?" Tamar asked.

¹⁷ *"I'll send you a young goat from my flock," Judah promised.*

"But what will you give me to guarantee that you will send the goat?" she asked.

¹⁸ *"What kind of guarantee do you want?" he replied.*

She answered, "Leave me your identification seal and its cord and the walking stick you are carrying." So Judah gave them to her. Then he had intercourse with her, and she became pregnant.

¹⁹ *Afterward she went back home, took off her veil, and put on her widow's clothing as usual.*

²⁰ *Later Judah asked his friend Hirah the Adullamite to take the young goat to the woman and to pick up the things he had given her as his guarantee. But Hirah couldn't find her.*

²¹ *So he asked the men who lived there, "Where can I find the shrine prostitute who was sitting beside the road at the entrance to Enaim?"*

"We've never had a shrine prostitute here," they replied.

²² So Hirah returned to Judah and told him, "I couldn't find her anywhere, and the men of the village claim they've never had a shrine prostitute there."
²³ "Then let her keep the things I gave her," Judah said. "I sent the young goat as we agreed, but you couldn't find her. We'd be the laughingstock of the village if we went back again to look for her."
²⁴ About three months later, Judah was told, "Tamar, your daughter-in-law, has acted like a prostitute. And now, because of this, she's pregnant."
"Bring her out, and let her be burned!" Judah demanded.

Wow! How hypocritical and self-righteous can a man be? To patronize the services of a prostitute then vehemently condemn a woman for being a prostitute! To the extent of demanding that the woman be put to death!

"Why such a callous reaction?" you may ask. Men tend to subconsciously overcompensate for their own shortcomings in dealing with other people's failures. Often, an attempt is made to cover up one's sinfulness by a severity in one's response to the sins of others. I am sure that you noticed the same negative behavior pattern in David in the story from 2 Samuel 12.

For as long as he thought that it was someone else involved, *"any man who would do such a thing deserves to die"* was David's judgment.

> ## *Men tend to subconsciously overcompensate for their own shortcomings in dealing with other people's failures.*

25 But as they were taking her out to kill her, she sent this message to her father-in-law: "The man who owns these things made me pregnant. Look closely. Whose seal and cord and walking stick are these?"
26 Judah recognized them immediately and said, "She is more righteous than I am, because I didn't arrange for her to marry my son Shelah." And Judah never slept with Tamar again.

Even though this poignant erotic story might sound like an episode from a contemporary soap opera, it certainly is from the Bible! When you read just this part of the story, it is not easy to understand Tamar's conduct. Rather, the effortless thing to do is to pass judgment on her and condemn her.

I did it for a good long time! I found fault with and condemned many things about my wife. This is because I insisted on looking at only a portion of the whole story! Over the years, I have also had the privilege to counsel with countless men who point fingers at their women. You will be hard-pressed to find enough men who would acknowledge that the women in their lives are merely a reflection of who they are! With all my confessions of believing the Bible to be the word of God, I still denied 1 Corinthians 11:7, where it is written, *"Woman reflects man's glory."*

Slightly over fifteen years ago, I attended a Family Conference in Denver, Colorado. One of the speakers at that conference was a very well-known Christian man. He is quite successful and highly respected as an expert in several different fields. I was not yet married at that time. I got married about a year and half after that conference. During the conference, the speaker made a statement that stuck with me. Addressing the men, the speaker said, "If your wife is not the woman you want her to be after five years of marriage, it is your own fault!"

> ## *The woman in your life reflects who you are.*

This statement really excited me. Something about the statement connected with me. At that time I could not identify what it was. In any case, I walked out of the conference with very high hopes.

Unfortunately, after about a couple of years of marriage, I began to seriously question that statement. As we neared five years of marriage, I began to begrudge the conference speaker! I started consoling myself by saying, "He could afford to speak like that simply because he just didn't know my wife!" After five years of marriage, I concluded that the speaker either made that statement up or he was just "blessed" to have a good wife!

Like many husbands, I could not see myself in my wife. I could not acknowledge my own contribution to what I perceived to be a mess! The same way that Tamar had indisputable evidence of Judah's ignorance, my wife could prove how I had turned her into the woman she had become. I was meeting myself daily, but I'm even humiliated to acknowledge that I could not recognize myself—notwithstanding my sincerity!

7

This is more like the story of the drunken man who one night was approached by the neighborhood policemen as he was frantically trying to unlock "his" front door. The policemen suspected that this intoxicated man was attempting to break into this house, even though the man kept insisting it was his own house. After a while, the man finally succeeded in unlocking the door somehow. As the policemen walked the man into the house, the man decided to demonstrate to them how much he knew the house and its contents. He went from room to room telling the policemen that he owned everything they were seeing in that house. When they finally made it to the main bedroom, the drunken man said, "If you still don't believe that this is my house, that woman sleeping in that bed is my wife, and that man sleeping next to her is me!"

When both Judah and David were confronted with the truth, they were able to courageously embrace it. I bet it was rough and humiliating, but they both did what they had to do. In every man's life there is that moment that is called a turning point. There is a night that is the beginning of a new day. In every man's life there is one night after which a glorious morning will come. My prayer for you is that right now may be that moment of truth for you.

Food For Thought

1. Can you see yourself in the women in your life?

2. How much do you want what you want? Tamar wanted a baby from Judah's family, and she did all that was in her power to get one! Could it be that Tamar knew God had promised that the Messiah was going to come through the linage of Judah? Could it be that she was so determined to take chances and possibly be the mother of the long-awaited Messiah?

3. Pay close attention to weaknesses in others that irritate you and honestly investigate why those particular weaknesses irritate you as much as they do.

4. If you happened to meet yourself, would you be willing to acknowledge yourself?

5. Pray that the spirit of truth will invade your life.

Chapter 2

There Never Was Such A Woman!

Being ignorant is not so much a shame,
as being unwilling to learn.—Benjamin Franklin

The claim made by the men of the village of Enaim that "there never was a prostitute there" is loaded with meaning. I've also heard this claim from a good number of in-laws when their son-in-law comes back to tell them the kind of person he thinks their daughter is. Many in-laws rightfully claim that they never had a daughter like that! The implication of the in-laws is that there is something that the son-in-law did or did not do that must have caused a radical change in their daughter. This is an allegation that many men dismiss with all the contempt that it deserves.

From the way Tamar negotiated the payment for her impending services to Judah, she really came across like a professional. It appears that even Judah got the satisfaction of knowing that he was not dealing with an amateur. In Judah's mind, the prostitute that he patronized must have been the talk of her village! That may be the reason why Judah didn't even think about the possibility of not ever finding this woman again. Like it is with many men,

Judah believed that what he saw in Tamar was actually the person Tamar was. In actuality Judah saw in Tamar the woman whom Judah and his sons made her to be!

So how was Tamar a reflection of Judah and his sons? How did they make her into the woman she became? Let us backtrack and look again at this sizzling Bible story. Let us now look at how the episode began. Let us go back to the R-rated chapter of the Bible that we read from earlier—Genesis 38—and let us begin at verse 6. Here is what it says:

"In the course of time, Judah arranged for his firstborn son, Er, to marry a young woman named Tamar." At this point it may be argued that Judah was simply playing the role of a father to his son. Arranged marriages were the norm in his culture.

"But Er was a wicked man in the LORD's sight, so the LORD took his life." It is very interesting to note how much parents can be committed to their children to the extent of failing to see their children's blunders. Everyone else minus the parents may notice the child's faults. In this case apparently God noticed something about Er that Judah, Er's father, did not necessarily see. If Judah saw the same thing that the Lord saw in Er, it would have been inexcusable for Judah to bring Tamar into that mess. Whatever it is that the Lord saw in Er, the Lord saw fit to take Er's life.

> [8] *Then Judah said to Er's brother Onan, "Go and marry Tamar, as our law requires of the brother of a man who has died. You must produce an heir for your brother."*
> [9] *But Onan was not willing to have a child who would not be his own heir. So whenever he had intercourse with his brother's wife, he spilled the semen on the*

*ground. This prevented her from having a child who
would belong to his brother.*

The Bible is very clear on what it is that Onan was not willing
to have: *"Onan was not willing to have a child who would not be
his own heir."* However, on the other hand, he sure was willing to
have sex with Tamar! Onan was willing to enjoy the pleasure of
sexual intercourse, but he did not want its fruit. The music was
enjoyable, but paying the piper was not desirable. It was a case of
saying yes to benefits and no to obligations. Consequently, Onan
figured that he could simply turn Tamar into a sexual object,
thereby beginning the process of changing Tamar's identity!

> ### *Don't expect to have benefits
> without any obligations.*

It is not implied in the Bible text that Onan was obliged to
marry his brother's wife. When this custom of marrying a brother's
widow was afterward made into law during the time of Moses, it
was made very clear that there was another option. Here is what
is written in Deuteronomy 25, from verse 5 to verse 9:

> [5] *If two brothers are living together on the same property
> and one of them dies without a son, his widow may
> not be married to anyone from outside the family.
> Instead, her husband's brother should marry her and
> have intercourse with her to fulfill the duties of a
> brother-in-law.*

> [6] *The first son she bears to him will be considered the son of the dead brother, so that his name will not be forgotten in Israel.*
> [7] *But if the man refuses to marry his brother's widow, she must go to the town gate and say to the elders assembled there, "My husband's brother refuses to preserve his brother's name in Israel—he refuses to fulfill the duties of a brother-in-law by marrying me."*
> [8] *The elders of the town will then summon him and talk with him. If he still refuses and says, "I don't want to marry her,"*
> [9] *the widow must walk over to him in the presence of the elders, pull his sandal from his foot, and spit in his face. Then she must declare, "This is what happens to a man who refuses to provide his brother with children."*

Therefore, it is plausible to conclude that Onan was under no obligation to marry his brother Er's wife. There is no mention made of any legal retribution. The only punishment mentioned was the act of being held up to public shame through the spitting-in-the-face and sandal-removing ritual! As such, Onan could have opted to leave Tamar alone. Unfortunately, Onan was a selfish man, and he thought he knew how to play "the game." He was merely concerned about having his sexual needs met. He had no regard for Tamar and her needs.

Unfortunately, many men are very selfish. Consider with me the story of Gerald and Erica, a couple now in their early fifties. They came to the North American continent over twenty years ago from Africa. Gerald was a student then. Erica worked hard to support her husband and their three sons. Sometimes she had to work two full-time jobs, not to mention being a full-time mother and wife! After his baccalaureate degree, Gerald went on to graduate school. After Gerald's first graduate degree, Erica thought it would be her turn to go school. To her surprise, when she brought up the issue to Gerald, she was told that there was no money for her to go to school! When Erica told me and my wife her story, Gerald was a recipient of three master's degrees and was working on his PhD. Erica was still hoping to matriculate some day.

Many men are selfish.

Onan's father, Judah, was also a very selfish man. He was more concerned about keeping a promise that he made to a "prostitute" so he could have his identification seal back than he was concerned about the promise he had made to his daughter-in-law to arrange that she marry his son Shelah. Tamar's own needs were not a priority to Judah and Onan.

It is very important to remember that from the very beginning, it was the man—Adam—who gave identity to everything that God brought under Adam's influence. This is what is written in Genesis chapter 2 verse 19: "*So the Lord God formed from the ground all the wild animals and all the birds of the sky. He brought them to the man to see what he would call them, and the man chose a name for each one.*" Then in verses 22 and 23 it says, "'*Then the Lord God made a woman from the rib, and he brought her to the man. "At last!" the man exclaimed. "This one is bone from my bone, and flesh from my flesh! She will be called 'woman,' because she was taken from 'man.'*'"

Therefore, we see that whatever Adam called what God brought to him is exactly what the thing became! Here is the principle to take note of and remember: All men are equipped by God to give identity to whatever God brings to them. This includes the women that God brings into the lives of all men.

> ### *All men are equipped by God to give identity to whatever God brings to them.*

When Tamar became part of Judah's household, she must have been an acceptable young lady. If it were not so, Judah would not have arranged for his son to marry her. Apparently, Judah and his sons were not cognizant of the fact that Tamar was simply raw material! During the time she was Onan's wife, Onan made Tamar into a sexual object. This is what Onan called Tamar in his own mind, and he sure treated her like a sexual object. In the process of time, Tamar became what Onan called her! Later on, when Tamar heard that Judah was taking a business trip to Timnah, Tamar planted herself in Judah's way *as* a sexual object. By this time, Tamar even knew how to dress for the job!

In my own life, I have observed that what I consistently say about my wife both in private and in public has direct bearing on how I treat her.

Just like in the banking system, how I treat my wife represents the deposits! It would be foolish of me to yell at my account for lacking more zeros at the end if I did not deposit the equivalent of those zeros into the account! It turns out that what I put in the account is what I can get out of the account—usually with compound interest!

When a man speaks about his woman, the man is basically speaking about himself! When a husband says his wife is a fool, either one of two things must be the case. It could be that the man is a bigger fool because he married a fool and did not even know at that time that he was marrying a fool. Or he married raw material that he made into a fool!

> ### *When a man speaks about his woman, he is basically speaking about himself.*

When Judah promised Tamar that he would send her a young goat from his flock as payment for the services Judah was asking for, Tamar was quick to ask for collateral. Why? Because Tamar knew that she was in the predicament that she was in because Judah had made a major promise to her before and Judah did not keep that promise. Tamar was not about to take another chance! It was Judah who gave Tamar the savvy to be a skillful negotiator.

I have had the privilege of listening to men from different walks of life matter-of-factly talk about their women. They have a way of demonizing their women while attempting to remove themselves from the equation. They try so very hard to exonerate themselves and assert that they do not see the elephant right in the center of their living room! Meanwhile, I have also had the pleasure of discovering, just like Hirah, that in the absence of these men, there really never were such women as they describe! For as long as Judah was not there, there was no prostitute in the village of Enaim.

As He did with Adam, God is still in the business of presenting things and people to man to see what man will name them. And whatever the name the man gives is what the objects become. My sincere prayer is that from this day forward, you will give only positive identity to everyone and everything God entrusts to you.

Food For Thought:

1. Judah potentially created a problem for his sons, even though that was not his intent.

2. For many men, a lot of problems would disappear from their lives if they remove selfishness.

3. What identity are you giving to people and things that God has brought to you?

4. When Tamar heard that Judah was taking a business trip to Timnah, she confidently planted herself in Judah's path. Apparently, she knew Judah much better than Judah cared to know her.

5. Pray that the Lord may deliver you from the lies that you tell yourself

Chapter 3

The Hirah Factor

Bad company corrupts good character.
—Apostle Paul

Even from a casual reading of Genesis 38, it is obvious that this fellow named Hirah was a very significant person in Judah's life. Genesis 38:12 refers to Hirah as Judah's friend. You may substitute Judah's name with yours and Hirah's name with Harry, Hasim, Hose, or Hozheri.

There are very few men who are fully conscious of it and will readily admit that their lives are undeniably shaped by their friends. Even though it is said in different ways that you become like your friends, many men still believe they can have the best of both worlds! They assume that they can hang out with whomever they want to hang out with and still maintain a strong moral life.

> **Your life is undeniably shaped by your friends.**

We are first introduced to Hirah at a time when Judah's life was headed in a wrong direction. In a fashion that is similar to how gangs influence people who are in trouble, Hirah became a dominant influence in "lonely" Judah's life. It is written in Genesis 38:1: *"And it came to pass at that time, that Judah went down from his brethren, and turned in to a certain Adullamite, whose name was Hirah"* (King James Version). Frequently, there are many well-meaning men who leave home and relocate to another town, state, country, or even continent. As life will have it, usually there is always a questionable character there to welcome them and keep them company.

It is not clear if Judah and Hirah were already acquaintances before Judah left home. One thing that is clear, though, from this verse is that Judah's life was declining. Judah was progressively sinking. Most of the time when the Bible highlights the fact that a person went down, trouble inevitably follows. For instance, Abram went down to Egypt, and there he ended up lying concerning his wife Sarai, saying she was his sister (Genesis 12:10–20). Samson went down to Timnath, and there he got involved with a Philistine woman (Judges 14). Jonah went down to Joppa to board a ship to Tarshish in an effort to run away from God's assignment (Jonah 1:2–3). Jonah soon found himself in the belly of a fish. A certain man went down from Jerusalem to Jericho and fell among thieves (Luke 10:30). I trust you get the picture! I also trust that you are not going down!

As a man, you know you are going down when you especially choose to surround yourself exclusively with people you like! It is clear from Genesis 38 that Judah liked Hirah. Judah possibly left his brothers in favor of Hirah. Friendship with Hirah was more important to Judah than his family. Even if Judah's brothers were not the best of company, Hirah was a poor substitute. Like all people, Judah did not have the privilege of choosing his family. However, he had the opportunity to choose his friends—and Judah chose Hirah!

It is interesting to note that Judah and Hirah were friends over a long period of time. They were friends before Judah married his Canaanite wife. Their friendship outlived Judah's marriage. They were friends after all of Judah's sons from this marriage were of marriageable age. All through this lengthy period of time, Hirah was a friend of choice to Judah.

The events of Genesis 38 validate that Hirah was the kind of friend who had a negative influence on Judah. Being in Adullam away from family worsened the situation for Judah. We are told that *"there he saw a Canaanite woman, the daughter of Shua, and he married her ..."* (Genesis 38:2). From the construction of the verse, it appears that this nameless woman's outward appearance may have been Judah's primary consideration in marrying her. He *saw* a Canaanite woman. Based on the fact that she was a Canaanite woman and Judah was an Israelite man, obviously, no spiritual considerations were taken into account. As such, Judah's choice would have been purely a physical one.

One of Judah's great descendants named Solomon later wrote, *"Charm is deceptive, and beauty does not last ..."* (Proverbs 31:30). If elegance is the principal quality that attracts a man to a woman, sooner or later, that man will be disappointed. Cuteness eventually evaporates as a vapor. However, a woman whose life is anchored in the Lord sustains her beauty.

Apart from making Jesus Christ the Lord of one's life, the choice of a mate is the most important decision that a person makes. The choice of a mate can accelerate or retard a man to his destiny. A man's rise or fall in life is interconnected to the kind of relationship he cultivates with his wife. As such, it is a decision that should be made with all due diligence. It certainly is a decision that should not be made lightly or unadvisedly. Whenever this decision is trivialized, a lot of trouble always ensues. A poor choice can effectively seal a man's fate!

From his marriage to the Canaanite woman, Judah had three sons. Two of the boys, named Er and Onan, were so wicked that God had to kill them! This is what is written:

> *6 In the course of time, Judah arranged for his firstborn son, Er, to marry a young woman named Tamar.*
> *7 But Er was a wicked man in the Lord's sight, so the Lord took his life.*
> *8 Then Judah said to Er's brother Onan, "Go and marry Tamar, as our law requires of the brother of a man who has died. You must produce an heir for your brother."*
> *9 But Onan was not willing to have a child who would not be his own heir. So whenever he had intercourse with his brother's wife, he spilled the semen on the ground. This prevented her from having a child who would belong to his brother.*
> *10 But the Lord considered it evil for Onan to deny a child to his dead brother. So the Lord took Onan's life, too.* (Genesis 38:6–10)

It is very difficult for some men to clearly see the negative influence of their friends on their lives for what it really is. This is because while their friends create problems for these men, those same friends are there for these men as they go through the problems! There is no question that Hirah was a major influence in Judah marrying a Canaanite woman. There should be no question that Canaanite influence played a significant part in how Judah's sons were raised. When Judah's wife and sons died, Judah turned to his buddy Hirah for comfort. Hirah was there for Judah. As negative as his influence on Judah was, Hirah was also there meeting Judah's companionship needs as well as he knew how. Hirah was more than willing to go with Judah on a business trip to Timnah just to spend time with him, to talk to him, and to help Judah cope with his situation. As such, it would have been very difficult for Judah to give a fair assessment of the kind of "friend" Hirah was to him.

In the end, Judah was behaving more like a Canaanite than an Israelite. Hirah was not behaving any more like an Israelite. It has already been noted that for Judah to get to where Hirah was, Judah had to go down! The root meaning of the word Canaan is "to be low or to be under." Hirah was a Canaanite.

Naturally, it is easier for the man who is down to pull the one who is up to come down to where he is. It is more difficult for the man who is up to pull the one who is down to where he is. The progress of most men is retarded because they waste time trying to pull up their so-called friends who are low down.

> ### *It is easier for the man who is down to pull the one who is up to come down to where he is.*

There is no record at all of Hirah ever—even remotely— persuading Judah to do anything that can be deemed constructive. Hirah's willingness to go and pay off a prostitute for Judah implies at least tacit approval of prostitution on his part. Chances are high that Hirah actually encouraged that kind of behavior. It appears that prostitution was possibly a part of Hirah's social circle and culture. Most of the time Hirah is mentioned in the Bible, the text is dealing with women!

There is at least one time that Hirah is mentioned in connection with the men of the village of Enaim. At that time, he was asking the men of Enaim where he could find "the prostitute." What guts? What made Hirah assume that these men would know? Because of his own involvement with prostitutes, Hirah assumed that these men were involved also. He thought fooling around was "a men thing." Like most men, Hirah consoled himself by believing that all men were like him.

> ## *Not all men patronize prostitutes.*

At least one young man had the nerve to say to his now-estranged wife after cheating on her, "Please don't hate me. I am just like every man. All men cheat one time or another!" These are words of a man who has no intentions of changing.

It should not require a rocket scientist to figure out how Judah wound up patronizing a prostitute. Judah was hanging out with the wrong company. He went down from his brethren (who were Israelites) and instead chose the company of an Adullamite (a pagan). This was a bad move morally and spiritually. From the writings of the Apostle Paul we are told that wrong friends will certainly produce wrong behavior patterns. It is written, *"Do not be misled: 'Bad company corrupts good character'"* (1 Corinthians 15:33). Your friends become your destiny.

Your friends become your destiny.

The choice of Hirah for a lifetime friend could possibly be the worst choice that Judah ever made. Judah chose to be his friend a guy he liked, a guy who had common interests, a guy who was always there for him, and a guy who was a comfortable and reliable companion. He chose a guy who was loyal to him. Hirah was a real friend. In fact, he was a real bad friend! He is a classic case of someone doing good while doing bad. It never works. Judah's closest friend was his worst enemy.

A man who will go and pay off a prostitute for you is not your friend. A man who will go buy drugs for you is not your friend. A man who will lie for you is not your friend. According to the wisdom of Solomon, a friend is supposed to sharpen his friend (Proverbs 27:17). A friend is supposed to be able to look you in your face and tell you the truth.

There had to be a reason for Judah to send Hirah to go and pay off the prostitute for him. Judah knew that he was not doing the right thing. That is why he would not exert extra effort to recover his important items from the prostitute. After one failed attempt, Judah was ready to quit. He said he did not want to be the laughingstock of the village.

This is like the story of the man who stole some valuable products and determined to sell them. He was already very excited just at the thought of how much money he was going to make out of the impending sale. Unfortunately, before he was able to sell the booty, someone else stole the loot from him! For obvious reasons, the man could not report this theft to the appropriate authorities. All he could do was to go around saying-stuff should not be like this in life!

Judah did not want to have to publicly confess that he patronized prostitutes. He found it easier to give up on his identification seal than to confront his wayward behavior and quit it. To seal his fate was a devil masquerading as a friend who was available to help him out. Judah, like many men, could use the advice of the prophet Micah when he wrote, *"Don't trust anyone—not your best friend ..."* (Micah 7:5).

Food For Thought

1. Do you realize that you are shaping someone else's life?

2. Can you stand people who tell you what you do not necessarily want to hear?

3. Who is influencing the major decisions that you make?

4. You may befriend whomever you choose! Just make sure that you have the dominance in moral issues.

5. You will never change behavior that you justify.

Chapter 4

Missed Opportunities

Opportunity is missed by most people because it is dressed in overalls and looks like work.—Thomas Alva Edison

"We stand by our product!" These words caught my attention when I saw them on a large billboard sign as I was driving in the Dallas area. It is a billboard sign sponsored by a company that makes copiers. What registered in my mind is that this company has utmost confidence in its product and is not ashamed whatsoever to be identified with it— no matter how it performs or what anyone else thinks about the product! In this day when recalls have become the main order of the day, I found this to be honorable. I was reminded of this billboard sign again when I thought of the Bible story of Tamar.

Tamar came out of God's factory as raw material. She entered into Judah's household as such, and the men in Judah's household abused her. After Er (Judah's first son) died, Judah treated Tamar according to the stipulations of his culture. Judah encouraged his second son, Onan, to marry Tamar. However, after Onan died, it appears that Judah succumbed to distrust. Internally, Judah started considering Tamar to be a possible cause for the death of his two sons Er and Onan. Instead of focusing on his sons, who apparently needed the attention, Judah shifted the blame to Tamar.

"I don't know why they blame everything on me," said Lynette, almost in tears. As difficult as it was, she went on to narrate how her in-laws blamed her for their son's demise. Everyone knew Marcus to have the ability to drink himself out of his mind regularly. His passion for life in the fast lane was an open secret. Marcus fathered two children with two other women. However, when Marcus's business collapsed, Lynette received the brunt of the blame for being a "gold digger."

This is the place where countless women regularly find themselves. They are severely emotionally distressed because after they are abused and subjected to all kinds of injustices, they are blamed for all of it. No one really wants to hear their side of the story. Instead of getting an apology, they are treated with suspicion. Instead of being comforted, they are blamed for losing their spouses.

Consider this incident that happened to a married couple, Laura and Wilson, while Ed, Wilson's younger brother, was staying with them. Ed got involved in a car accident on the way from work. The following day, Ed and Wilson arranged to take Ed's car to a local collision repair center for the necessary repairs. The two brothers agreed that while Ed's car was at the collision repair center, Ed would be driving Laura's other car. When Ed went to ask for the spare key, Laura was more surprised than she was upset. However, when Laura asked her husband why she was not consulted about the matter, Wilson snapped at his wife, accusing her of not wanting to help his brother out!

To make matters worse, most of these women find themselves locked into situations that deny them progress. Tamar was locked into a lose-lose situation. She was made to wait for Shelah, Judah's third son, who never came. Meanwhile, she could not legally marry anyone else. She could not move on with her life. Tamar was stuck. At least that is how it appeared in the natural realm.

The beauty of life that is hidden from many men and women lies in the fact that the way things appear in the natural realm is not final! The men in Tamar's life wrote her off as a sexual object. That is how she looked to them. Tamar's manufacturer, God Incorporated, knew the product better than these men! As bleak as the situation appeared, at the risk of ruining His reputation, God stepped into Tamar's situation and stood by His product! He turned what appeared in the physical realm to be a period into a comma! God exercised His sovereignty and promoted what was relegated to a sex object into a royal ornament.

> ## *Things are never as they appear.*

Unlike all of us, God had the chance to choose His own natural parents! He selected the people whom he wanted to be in the family tree of Jesus. Of all the people God could choose from, He chose Tamar! While Judah probably suspected Tamar of possibly having a jinx that killed her two husbands, Er and Onan, God saw significant value in Tamar, and He did not miss the opportunity to salvage this diamond in the rough when she was trashed. Here is what is recorded by Matthew, the Gospel writer, in chapter 1:1–3, *"This is a record of the ancestors of Jesus the Messiah, a descendant of David and of Abraham: Abraham was the father of Isaac. Isaac was the father of Jacob. Jacob was the father of Judah and his brothers. Judah was the father of Perez and Zerah (whose mother was Tamar) ..."*

From that one-night stand with Judah on the road near the village of Enaim, Tamar became pregnant. *"When the time came for Tamar to give birth, it was discovered that she was carrying twins"* (Genesis 38:27). The boys were named Perez and Zerah.

Oh, that men would be warned that in many cases, all it takes is just one time to mess up one's life.

> ***All it takes is just one time to mess up your life.***

It is noteworthy that Judah missed the opportunity to properly support a woman who was carrying his twin boys during her pregnancy. One of the reasons Judah missed this opportunity is because he was a pretender. Do you still remember that big show Judah put up just before Tamar produced undeniable evidence that Judah was the man who impregnated her?

In any case, this was not the first opportunity that Judah missed. Before this, Judah was presented with a once-in-a-lifetime opportunity to train his sons, particularly Er and Onan. Unfortunately, that opportunity was also missed. Instead, occasion was taken to transfer the needed focus on their shortcomings to blaming Tamar. As a result, Judah's sons did not receive the help they desperately needed, and Tamar was unnecessarily wounded emotionally, thereby creating another no-win situation. Her emotional condition would further present some challenges as she raised her twin sons (Perez and Zerah) possibly as a single mother.

Just like his father, Onan missed several opportunities. Obviously, he missed the opportunity to develop a possible meaningful relationship with Tamar. This set him on a downward spiral. Onan went on to miss the opportunity to produce an heir for his late elder brother, Er. While he was at it, Onan missed the opportunity to continue in his own personal growth and development.

When Judah encouraged him to marry Tamar, Onan could have seized the opportunity and let his father know that he had no interest in that arrangement. Instead, Onan compounded the pretending spirit of his father and took it to the next level. He wound up being a classical pretender. He pretended that he was an upholder of his culture. Onan also pretended that he was doing his duty as required of him by the law and possibly received all the accompanying merits. Meanwhile, he was busy deceiving his father and defrauding Tamar.

Oh, how about our friend Wilson? Was his response to the question from his wife, Laura, warranted? Was that not another missed opportunity? Did he not miss an opportunity to work as a team with his wife? Did not life present Wilson with an opportunity to be humble and apologize to his wife for overlooking her in the discussion and planning process? What an opportunity that was for Wilson to improve on his communication skills.

Unfortunately, all this truly sounds like too much work to many men. In the words of Henry Ford, "whether you think you can or you think you can't—you are right!"

It is my conviction that if Judah and his sons had known Tamar the same way that God knew her, they would have treated her differently. As a community of men, small as it was, these men missed an opportunity to treat Tamar like who she really was—royalty! Well, she is a link in the ancestry of Jesus—the King of kings. Royalty par excellence!

One of the well known and outstanding clerics in my city married a single mother who earlier on in her life was dumped by another man. Amazingly, alongside her new husband, this same woman who was once written off is flourishing tremendously.

> *Opportunity is missed by most people because it is dressed in overalls and looks like work.*

Many men miss the opportunity to treat their women with the dignity and honor that they deserve because they really do not know the product in their hands! Because of this ignorance, they call the product by the wrong name and abuse it. When they get unfavorable results, they simply blame the product. The opportunity to really know the product and enjoy it is usually missed. Above all, these men miss the opportunity to look into their own lives and address their inadequacies.

It has been said that the face of opportunity is unattractive and its backside is slippery. Once you let it pass you by, it is difficult to grab hold of it later. May your life not be a chronicle of missed opportunities ...

Food For Thought

1. Judah was not a failure in helping his sons until he started blaming Tamar for his sons' demise. In life you can fail many times. You are not a failure until you start blaming someone else for your failures.

2. Judah created a situation that denied Tamar progress, even though it was in the power of his hands to pave the way to Tamar's success.

3. Someone else may gladly receive what you are calling trash and demonstrate that it is in fact treasure.

4. Do not let anyone besides God write the final chapter of your life.

5. Pray that the Lord will open your eyes to see the hidden opportunities in your life.

Chapter 5

DIY

Seldom does an individual exceed his own expectations.
—Unknown

One of the many concepts that I was confronted with when I came to the United States is DIY. Yes, you got it right—it means *do it yourself*! Coming from a background characterized by housemaids, garden boys, and gas station attendants, I was totally blown away by the thought of purchasing components of a desk in a box allowing me to go home and assemble the desk on my own. This was really a wow idea to me. I jumped on the opportunity, and fifteen years later, I still cherish that first piece of furniture that I put together with my own hands! All of a sudden, I realized that I could possibly do most of the things that for all my life I had relied on other people to do for me.

God equipped man with DIY capabilities, and then He blessed man with the work to do as well as all the needed equipment and material for the work. Contrary to what most people believe, work is a blessing and not a curse. According to the record of scripture, God gave Adam work before sin and the ensuing curse ever came into the picture. This is what is written, *"The Lord God placed the man in the Garden of Eden to tend and watch over it"* (Genesis 2:15). Tending and watching over the Garden of Eden was work.

Work is a blessing, not a curse.

There are different types of work that God provided for man to do. Building a marital relationship is one type of work that God gave to man.

Almost all couples that I know agree on the fact that building a marriage is in fact full-time work! Even though they may work at it on a part-time basis, they are aware that marriage needs full-time attention. The disagreement is mainly on who is supposed to do what in building up the marriage?

Marriage is full-time work.

Many male pundits, counselors, psychologists, and even clerics take the position that the woman is responsible for the outcome of the project. This position is established almost as a norm even in our times. M. Gary Neuman's celebrated book, *The Truth About Cheating*, is one typical example.

There are yet others who are "more righteous" than this first group. Those in this camp take a more palliative position and insist that building up a marriage should be a fifty-fifty effort between a husband and a wife.

I find it interesting that the One who instituted marriage takes a different position from Mr. Neuman and all those who belong to

Mr. Neuman's tribe as well as those in the more righteous camp. Marriage is not a product of society. It was manufactured by "God Incorporated." Jesus settled this issue of custody for marriage in Matthew 19:4–8. The passage is a record of what was intended to be a trap for Jesus. Some Pharisees went to Jesus and questioned Him about divorce. In response, Jesus talked to them about marriage! Jesus very wisely told His audience on that occasion that divorce is not the issue that needs attention. The issue that needs to be addressed is marriage. God instituted marriage, and it was man who came up with divorce! Without marriage there is no divorce.

Before He was a Marriage Officer, God was a Planner. Every activity of God is calculated. Again, Genesis 2:15 tells us what God did before He presented the woman to the man. Here is what is written: *"The Lord God placed the man in the Garden of Eden to tend and watch over it."*

This was a foundational act by God. This was preparing the man to know how to handle the woman when she would later be presented to him. The word *tend* in this verse is an interpretation of a Hebrew word that means to till the land or to cultivate. According to the Merriam-Webster Online dictionary, to cultivate is "to foster growth; to improve by labor, care or study." Cultivate also means to refine.

So what we see from the Bible is that God equipped the man with the ability to develop his environment. That is also why God intentionally placed the man in an environment where there was provision for the man to work. Man was not only equipped with the ability to work—he was given a mandate to work. With all the wonderful things that Eden was, it also was an environment that required the man to improve it. Eden was a DIY type of environment. Eden could use some refining! Eden was also an environment that could be deteriorated. Meanwhile, all that the man needed was provided for him—only some assembling was required! Keep in mind that this was before the woman was formed!

What is clearly revealed in the Bible is that from the very inception, God never gave the man a finished product. God did not give the man a computer. Instead, God gave the man brains and mineral resources! The man is supposed to improve by labor, care, or study the environment that God puts the man in. A deteriorating environment is a clear sign that the man involved is malfunctioning. The way to improve a deteriorating environment is to fix the man—not to put the man in a different environment.

Evidently, God intentionally gave the woman to the man as an unfinished product! This is what qualifies her as raw material. God left a lot of room for the man to cultivate the woman, and not vice versa. Unfortunately, many women are uncultivated by their men! When weeds of life begin to choke up these women, the first people to complain are the men. There are all kinds of weeds that can choke up a woman. These weeds are in fact flowers whose virtues have not been drawn out.

> ### *God never gave the man a finished product.*

When the woman is properly cultivated by her man, she will turn around and be an indescribable blessing to the man. On the other hand, when proper effort is not put into cultivating her, the woman malfunctions to varying degrees. In any case, whether she becomes a blessing or a burden, as a husband, you do it yourself.

I have a friend who in the past several years has been making admirable strides in the areas of business and management. He owns a viable garment manufacturing company. He is also in the highest tier of management of a group of companies headquartered in New England.

Not too long ago, his wife of almost ten years walked out on him. Talking to me one day he said, "It amazes me that I have not been able to employ in my own marriage the principles that have worked so well for me in business." My friend said that at work he knows that he should "never attack an employee's self-worth but merely address the problem. However at home I do the exact opposite. I attack my wife and not the problem. As a result, I am doing great in business and dismally in my relationship with my wife!"

During that conversation, we agreed that he would begin to apply some of the principles in his marriage. It did not take long for him to experience an almost 180-degree turn around in his marriage.

The man has to take the initiative to foster growth in the woman. This building up of the woman by the man has to be done with understanding. It also has to be done with intentionality and with consistency. This is a type of work that has to be done both in private and in public. It has to go way beyond sweet talking at particular times of the night or day in order to get a service from her! It has to become a lifestyle.

> *The man has to take the initiative to foster growth in the woman.*

When cultivating your woman becomes your typical way of life, a healthy measure of emotional stability is created in your relationship. The emotional stability of a relationship between a husband and wife should not be left up to chance or to the fluke of nature. It is something that the man can directly influence and control.

A woman who receives regular generous portions of praise and admiration from her man will have healthy self-esteem. It is said that the number one complaint of most married women is not the absence of romantic love, finances, or even conflict with the in-laws but low self-esteem. It is the sense of feeling unloved and unlovable. This is a clear indication that a vast majority of men are not working like they are supposed to.

God, the One who instituted marriage, knows how serious and important this type of work is. According to God's estimation, a newly married man needs at least a whole year of building a strong foundation for cultivating his woman emotionally. This is why it is written in Deuteronomy 24:5, "*A newly married man must not be drafted into the army or be given any other official responsibilities. He must be free to spend one year at home, bringing happiness to the wife he has married.*" This would prepare the two for a life of joy and stability.

I have learned many great and priceless lessons from my own relationship with my wife. I have observed that for as long as she has the assurance of my love, admiration, and support, she can pretty much deal with all the other battles of life as they come. In the past I saw her struggle a great deal when I was not forthcoming in affirming and cherishing her as I was supposed to.

Interestingly, when most men are trying to "get" a woman, they maximize on boosting her self-esteem. She is the cutest. She is altogether smart. She dresses better than every other woman.

Indeed, all her clothes appear to be tailor-made. Even her very gait is gracious! She is simply the best. Here some roses. There some chocolates and other additional goodies! Now, because she has capacity to be cultivated, this works on the woman like magic. As a result, she gives in to you without reservation.

> ### *When most men are trying to "get" a woman, they maximize on boosting her self-esteem.*

Then after you get her, you stop building her up. It may not be intentional with some men. However, with others it is a clear symptom of their conquest mentality—the mindset to do whatever it takes to win. Once they win, they aim at something else to win.

In any case, when you stop building her up, she starts malfunctioning, and you get frustrated. Instead of accusing her, why don't you start working again and resume building her up from where you left off the project and go full throttle?

- ➢ Become generous in complimenting her.

- ➢ Give her a lot of affection and attention.

- ➢ Involve her in all your endeavors.

- ➢ Appreciate her and buy her flowers (not just on Valentine's Day).

- ➢ Call her and talk to her throughout the day.

- ➢ Help her with the children.

> ➤ Listen to her.

> ➤ Provide for her needs (spiritual, emotional, physical, and material)

> ➤ Constantly assure her of your commitment to be with her.

> ➤ Always guarantee her of your dedication to build her up.

> ➤ Publicly speak well of her all the time.

> ➤ Privately express your need for her.

Being the incomparable Planner that He is, God made Eve and wired her to accomplish a very specific assignment in relationship to Adam. *Then the Lord God said, "It is not good for the man to be alone. I will make a helper who is just right for him"* (Genesis 2:18).

God equipped the man to work and blessed him with the work. Then God proposed to provide the man with a helper. God provided Eve to help Adam in his work. However, in order for Eve to efficiently help Adam, it was Adam who had to first help her! Adam had to teach Eve everything he knew and assure her that she could do it. That pattern has not changed. Help produces help! A man's happiness and success in marriage is a by-product of his conscious efforts to build up his woman.

If you happen to be the one asking how long is justifiable for you to build your woman up before you see tangible results, I thank you for asking! Allow me to say that the assignment to build up your woman is not a timed contract. It is an obligation you have to perform because it is the right thing to do and not because you expect a certain response by a particular time. It is about the attitude of your heart more than it is about the response of the other party involved.

Incidentally, treating someone a certain way in order to get a favorable response constitutes a form of exploitation. And sad to say, many husbands exploit their wives.

Are you an exploiter?

When you do what you need to do for the right reasons, your experience will go beyond your expectations—guaranteed! Meanwhile, a delayed response from your wife will not derail you. However, when this kind of understanding and resolve is missing from the man, the woman involved intuitively picks it up and consequently withholds her full cooperation with the man to the frustration of both of them.

It is only unfortunate that a vast number of men are afraid of commitment. They are afraid of committing themselves to the task of building up their women. They are afraid of committing to a job, a church, or even to themselves! Many men are scared to death of interactions that are dominated by obligations.

It is this lack of commitment that says we can simply cohabit. We can have all the desirable benefits of companionship, but let us never talk about marriage.

Most men are afraid of commitment.

Commitment goes beyond staying together for life. People can stay together for life because of constraints and not necessarily because they are committed to each other. Constraints are the things that accumulate as a relationship grows and make it hard to break up. Things such as financial considerations, responsibilities for children, social pressure, personal image, or a lack of foreseeable viable alternatives are good examples of constraints. Are you committed?

From the very inception, God never envisioned a marriage without the component of oneness! It is written, *"Male and female created he them; and blessed them, and called their name Adam, in the day when they were created"* (Genesis 5:2). It is very important to note that God blessed a team not an individual! Oneness in marriage attracts the blessings of God. On the other hand, it doesn't matter how hard individuals try separately, Jesus already gave His word concerning disunity: *"A house divided against itself shall not stand"* (Matthew 12:25).

> ### In the beginning, God blessed a team not an individual.

Man, God knows that you need help! It is an open secret. You have nothing to lose by being truthful and humbly letting your woman know that you need her help. To the contrary, you have everything to gain! When you effectively help her to help you—with God's blessing—you become an invincible team. *"A person standing alone can be attacked and defeated, but two can stand back-to-back and conquer. Three are even better, for a triple-braided cord is not easily broken"* (Ecclesiastes 4:12).

Over the years, man has applied the DIY principle to home improvement, car maintenance, publishing books, and much more. The time has come to aggressively apply the principle where it matters the most—in marriage. That is how God designed marriage to function. You—man—have to make it work.

The woman you have is the very best you could do when you got her. Now do your best with what you have. Changing raw material is not the answer. You need to work with what you already have. I believe it was Stephen Kaggwa who said, "Successful people aren't born that way. They become successful by doing things unsuccessful people don't like to do. The successful people don't always like these things themselves; they just get on and do them!" Why don't you just get on and start cultivating your woman? Get on and become yet another success story.

Food For Thought

1. You are able to do much more than you know.

2. Without hard work, nothing but weeds freely grow in a field.

3. Every man who has what it takes to successfully court a girl into marriage also has what it takes to keep that marriage rocking.

4. Why do you do the good things that you do?

5. Every man is a teacher.

Chapter 6

Exempli Gratia

I think the greatest way to learn is to learn by someone's example.—Tobey Maguire

"The most difficult part about what you are teaching us is that I never saw my parents model it when I was growing up!" This statement was made by one man during a marriage enrichment session that my wife and I were conducting not too long ago. The man went on to say, "Growing up, I never heard my father compliment my mother in public. I don't ever remember seeing him express affection to my mother." Right then I knew that this man was speaking on behalf of many other men.

As a result, we spent a portion of the time looking at the example of the greatest husband there has ever been—Jesus Christ! We looked at these verses found in the book of Ephesians 5:25–31:

> *25 For husbands, this means love your wives, just as Christ loved the church. He gave up his life for her*

26 to make her holy and clean, washed by the cleansing of God's word.

27 He did this to present her to himself as a glorious church without a spot or wrinkle or any other blemish. Instead, she will be holy and without fault.

28 In the same way, husbands ought to love their wives as they love their own bodies. For a man who loves his wife actually shows love for himself.

29 No one hates his own body but feeds and cares for it, just as Christ cares for the church.

30 And we are members of his body.

31 As the Scriptures say, "A man leaves his father and mother and is joined to his wife, and the two are united into one."

The first thing that is clear from this passage is the fact that a husband is under commandment to love his wife. It is not a suggestion! It is an obligation that has to be satisfied. Love is clearly a verb. It is a doing word. When a husband obeys the command to love his wife, if the feelings were not present starting out, they definitely follow! Consequently, the feelings end up being a part of the husband as he lives in obedience to the commandment to love his wife.

> ### *A husband is under commandment to love his wife.*

I am fascinated by cultures that have arranged marriages. A young man and a young woman are put together, and they are supposed to learn to love each other. Interestingly, the divorce rate in these cultures is lower than in other cultures.

When a man is not fond of his wife, he is violating a commandment of God! This is a violation that is costly. In the words of the Apostle Peter, failure of a husband to dwell with his wife according to knowledge causes that husband's line of communication with God to be cut off (1 Peter 3:7)! This places the husband in a position where he cannot legally access God. A man who is cut off from God is a man who is vulnerable.

God calls for deep love out of the husband because God knows that He put it in there! It would be unfair and unreasonable for God to command the man to do something that the man is incapable of doing. As such, we have to conclude that it is possible for a husband to love his wife dearly.

This is contrary to some of the teachings that I heard from my own pastor when I was a teenager! On several occasions my senior pastor would say to us, "There is a way to tell if the woman in the passenger seat of a car is the man's wife or his girlfriend. If she looks straight ahead as they talk, she is his wife. If they look at each other and smile as they talk and they are close to each other—no doubt, she is his girlfriend!" According to him, it is mutually exclusive for a woman to be a wife and receive public affection from her husband.

For all of us men who were not privileged to see our biological fathers or spiritual fathers model the right things, we are instructed to observe the example of Christ instead. We are supposed to love our wives just as Christ loves His wife—the church.

How does Christ love the church? He is committed to the church. He gives the church all His focus and attention. Christ does this by reaching out to her and giving the church something that is a necessity to her. The church needs salvation in order for her to be complete and blossom. The husband should commit himself to his wife and reach out to her by giving her the love that she needs to flourish.

Christ loves the church unconditionally. Christ's love toward the church is not based on the church's spiritual condition or her behavior and attitude toward Christ. It is love that has no qualifications. This is the kind of love that a husband is obligated to have toward his wife.

> ## *A husband's love for his wife must be unconditional.*

I find it amazing that Christ refines the church "by the cleansing of God's word …" Etymologically; *word* means "that which is or has been uttered by a living voice." It means something spoken.

The complaint that I hear from an untold number of wives is that their husbands just won't talk! Meanwhile, the wife needs verbal communication from her husband. Christ's dealings with His wife validate this position.

May I challenge all husbands to learn from the best? Christ spoke to His wife, and He still does. When He was here on earth, Christ spoke to His disciples regardless of the situation they were in. For instance, when the disciples were fearful, Jesus strengthened them by saying, "Don't be afraid" or "Take courage." When they were in doubt, Jesus encouraged them by saying, "Do not be faithless—simply believe." There is power that is not to be minimized in a word that is fitly spoken.

> ## *When a man won't talk, the woman involved feels shut out and frustrated.*

Wives work very well when they are spoken to as much as possible by their husbands. It helps them to feel better connected to their husbands. It also helps them to feel secure. They feel vulnerable, incapacitated, and weak when they have to deal with a man who will not disclose what he is thinking—a man who won't talk. When a man won't talk, the woman involved feels shut out and frustrated because God wired her to be a helper.

There is a specific reason Christ works hard at refining His wife. Christ wants to be able to stand by His wife without shame some day!

Just like every husband, Christ was not presented with a perfect wife. To the contrary, Christ's wife—the church—has all kinds of faults and blemishes. Meanwhile, Christ's job is to refine the church, molding her into the wife that He desires. In His mind, Christ has an ideal wife that He desires. He is working hard to bring out that wife from the raw material that is available to Him. What a powerful demonstration of the do-it-yourself concept! From the raw material that is available to him, every husband should work hard to produce for himself a wife he will be proud to stand next to.

A word of counsel to all future husbands reading these pages: You will be prudent to espouse these principles and apply them to your marriage from the front end as much as possible. You are better off implementing the principles from the beginning instead of trying to heal an already embittered marriage.

It is difficult to ignore the emphasis on the genitive case used in the verses above. Husbands ought to love their *own* wives and not someone else's wife! The church is Jesus's wife. The place of employment is someone else's gal!

It is amazing to see what a man is prepared to do for a woman as long as she is not his wife. It is effortless to call and send text messages or e-mails. He does not have to think twice about driving across town to go and have lunch with her. There is nothing too expensive. He is almost always available. For some reason the love just flows out.

The Bible does not try to hide the fact that "stolen water is sweet!" However, it also makes it clear that there is destruction that follows the sweetness. The instruction of scripture is that love should be directed to a husband's *own* wife.

If you take the time to read carefully the instructions on how to "operate" wife, this is what you will find: "This product will permanently change your life for better or for worse. For maximum performance, please nourish, nurture, and properly support constantly. Always pay attention and handle with care. Keep under warmth of tender loving care at all times. Foster growth with affection. Warnings: Neglect or haphazard application of the above will cause product to develop complications. Do not engage product if you are not committed. When operating this product, do not expect symptoms to disappear after a couple of trials. Do not ever discard!"

> *Giving up on your wife equals giving up on yourself.*

The language of the Bible connotes that a husband actually has to bring his wife up! This is a job that no one else can effectively do.

A woman's father may raise her, and the woman's husband must bring her up to the level that the husband desires. If the husband does not, he will ultimately lose because he will be busy fighting against himself. The wife is an integral part of the husband. Giving up on her is giving up on self. For a husband who loves his wife actually shows love for himself.

I find Paul's declaration that *"no one hates his own body"* to be very intriguing. I would think that people who abuse their bodies actually hate their bodies, but Paul said it is not so. Speaking by the spirit of God, Paul said even those people still nourish their bodies with a meal and a bath sometimes! They still care for their bodies by giving them protection from the elements. Similarly, every husband has to bring up his wife to maturity.

Christ does not expect us men to learn from Him just by precept but also by example. He has told us by precept how husbands need to handle their wives. What a great lesson He demonstrated to us when He left His Father in heaven and came to earth to pursue His bride—the church! According to what is written in Ephesians 5:31, a man has to free himself from his father and mother in order for him to do his job well. For as long as a man is still under the domain of his parents, he will not be able to fully develop into the husband that God requires the man to be.

The Bible mandates the man to leave his father and mother for a very clear reason. The Apostle Paul expressed the reason in a very powerful and picturesque way. The man is to be joined to or cleave to his wife. This means that the man is to glue himself to his wife. The husband does this by actively pursuing his wife and staying close to her until they are united into one. A husband does not become one flesh with his wife by being passive. This is an assignment that calls for determination and knowledge. Becoming one flesh has nothing to do with sex.

The phrase "leave his father and mother" is in reference to more than just geographical relocation. Some men live in different continents from their parents, but the word of their parents is what prevails in their homes! No wonder their marriages are pathetic.

One of the most formidable obstacles that many men have to overcome is tradition. Matthew, the Gospel writer, one day captured a very interesting incident in Matthew 15:1-3: *"Some Pharisees and teachers of religious law now arrived from Jerusalem to see Jesus. They asked him, "Why do your disciples disobey our age-old tradition? For they ignore our tradition of ceremonial hand washing before they eat." Jesus replied, "And why do you, by your traditions, violate the direct commandments of God?"*

> **Tradition is a formidable obstacle that many men need to overcome.**

From Jesus's response, we can see that the Pharisees had only presented one side of an issue. They only talked about Jesus's disciples' disobedience of tradition. They did not say anything about what the disciples were obeying. Jesus highlights the truth that it is not what you stand for that is critical but what you stand against. The Pharisees stood for their traditions but against the commandments of God.

Unfortunately, there are many men who are in that same position today. They would rather be custodians of man-made traditions than followers of truth. As a man, you can know with certainty if you are holding on to your traditions or pursuing the truth. When you are offended by the truth, it is an indication that you are holding tightly to that which you have always known. You are in love with your traditions.

During this confrontation with the Pharisees and teachers of religious law, Jesus gave some insight into the real problem. Jesus said, *"These people honor me with their lips, but their hearts are far from me. Their worship is a farce, for they teach man-made ideas as commands from God"* (Matthew 15:8–9). It is not so much about a man's traditions as much as it is about the man's heart. Who or what is the man's heart given to? His lips may say all the right things, but his heart may be someplace else.

To a very large extent, Albert Schweitzer was right when he said, "Example is not the main thing in influencing others; it is the only thing." The statement that was made by the man in the marriage enrichment session that I mentioned earlier concurs with this truth. His tradition negated the truth that he was hearing, but his heart was open to the truth. The man needed someone he could point to and say, "exempli gratia!" This is the way to say "for example" in Latin. Thanks to God for Christ—the paragon of what a husband should be like!

Food For Thought

1. When a husband obeys the command to love his wife, if the feelings were not present starting out, they definitely follow!

2. The love that a husband should have for his wife is not primarily sexual.

3. One does not have to be talkative to be a good communicator.

4. The perfect wife that you desire does exist. She exists in only one place—your mind! Your job is to work her out of your mind into reality.

5. Do you have the courage to break away from your traditions in favor of the truth?

Chapter 7

Unmasking The Real Problem

*And you will know the truth, and the truth
will set you free.*—Jesus Christ

Lack of desire to know the truth carries repercussions. In our story from Genesis 38, Judah comes across as a man who did not care to know the truth.

This was the case when his two sons Er and Onan died consecutively. It was convenient for Judah to victimize his daughter-in-law instead of diligently searching after the truth about the matter. Later on, when Judah patronized the woman he thought to be a prostitute, Judah had no interest whatsoever in knowing the woman who was behind the veil! Consequently, Judah impregnated his own daughter-in-law. It is unfortunate that many husbands are sex addicts who have no desire to truly know their wives.

> *Lack of desire to know the
> truth carries repercussions.*

Note also that when Hirah, Judah's friend, gave Judah the report of his failure to find the woman who had in her custody the equivalents of Judah's driver's license, social security card, and credit card, Judah apparently made light of the report. No serious thought was given to any possible implications of Hirah's findings.

It is my trust that you have read this far in this book because you have a deep yearning to know the truth. My prayer for you is that your desire may be granted. May the Spirit of truth invade your life—in the name of Jesus.

Even a casual reading through the Bible will show that marriage is not a peripheral issue in God's plan for humanity. To the contrary, it is clear that marriage is of great value, and it is also at the center of God's plan. The author of the book of Hebrews commands us to *"give honor to marriage ..."* (Hebrews 13:4).

It should not be considered coincidental that in the book of beginnings—Genesis—there is a record of the institution of marriage between a man and a woman, and in the last book—Revelations—there is an account of the vision of the marriage supper of the Lamb. In that ceremony, Jesus Christ will be the Bridegroom and the universal church will be the bride.

Throughout the Old Testament, God's love for His people is depicted as the love of a husband for his wife. This is what is written in the book of Hosea 2:19–20: *"I will make you my wife forever, showing you righteousness and justice, unfailing love and compassion. I will be faithful to you and make you mine, and you will finally know me as the Lord."* God's eternal plan is to be married to His people forever.

In the New Testament, Jesus Christ embodies this love. In the book of Ephesians 5:31–32, the Apostle Paul lets us know that marriage signifies the great union that is between Christ and His church. Here is what Paul says: *"As the Scriptures say, 'A man leaves his father and mother and is joined to his wife, and the two are united into one.' This is a great mystery, but it is an illustration of the way Christ and the church are one."*

Paul rightfully calls this union a mystery. Unfortunately, the devil has managed to sell the lie that anyone who is above a certain age or can perform sexually understands marriage. Consequently, a vast number of people completely miss what marriage is about.

Marriage is about the eternal plan of God to be married to His people forever. To all people, at all times, marriage is supposed to be a daily reminder of the destiny of the universal church—the bride of Christ. Our destiny is to be united with Christ eternally. As such, marriage is very important to God.

It so happens that whatever is important to God is also important to God's archenemy—the devil! As such, marriage is very important to the devil. Satan saw God's blueprint, and he knows the plan of God and the destiny of mankind. Bear in mind that Lucifer (satan) used to live in heaven before he was kicked out because of insubordination. Part of satan's present mission is to fight the plan that God has for humanity.

> **Whatever is important to God is important to the devil.**

Some of the devil's methods of fighting the plan of God include either distorting or destroying marriages. A destroyed marriage seeks to negate the validity of God's promise to marry His people forever. It is a mockery to the idea of permanency in marriage. A distorted marriage does not properly signify or reflect the relationship that is between Christ and the church.

Item number one on the devil's agenda is to ascertain that the husband is ignorant of or confused about his God-given bedrock job of bringing his wife up. Once the man is out of place, the woman and the children are also displaced. When the foundation is compromised, whatever is built upon it is bound to collapse. Human society is in great turmoil because the foundation of human society is deeply fractured. Because the man has either been distracted from or has completely given up on his primary assignment, his other labors have become misplaced. Unfortunately, this is what many men do not comprehend.

I listened intently as thirty-two-year-old Brandon narrated to me the story of his relationship with Shawntrice and how they wound up filing for a divorce after six years of marriage. He told me how he used to spend quality time with his then girlfriend and take her skating and to watch movies and the like. How he married her right after her college graduation. Then how because Shawntrice could not find a "professional job" in her field of study right after graduation, Brandon decided to take a second job in order to "pay all the bills." He never could understand why his wife started and kept on talking against the change of his focus from her as a person to paying bills. Meanwhile, he started feeling unappreciated. She did not appreciate the house he bought for them to live in. Brandon soon concluded that his wife severely lacked gratitude, and he developed bitterness against her. He was fully convinced that he had invested 200 percent into the marriage! Self-righteously, Brandon asked me the question, "What could I have done differently?" This gave me an opportunity to instruct Brandon on what his primary assignment as a husband should have been. Unfortunately, his marriage had already collapsed.

Many misguided men are busy with numerous secondary enterprises. They still try to build all kinds of fancy marital structures on faulty foundations or directly on the sand! They try to build on money, popularity, common sense, or human intelligence. All these are recipes with all the ingredients for disaster. The structures that they build cannot stand against the floods and strong winds of life. Whenever the building of a marriage collapses, the devil is always pleased.

> ### *Many misguided men are busy with numerous secondary enterprises.*

Commitment to building a strong and stable marriage at whatever cost thwarts satan's plan and upholds God's plan. A marriage is not about a husband and a wife! A marriage is about the plan of God versus the plan of satan. The truth about marriage is that it is a spiritual battle! The fighting is not *"against flesh-and-blood enemies, but against evil rulers and authorities of the unseen world, against mighty powers in this dark world, and against evil spirits in the heavenly places"* (Ephesians 6:12).

> ### *Marriage is a spiritual battle.*

Ignorance of this truth is what causes married men to fight wrong enemies and wrong battles. A husband will unknowingly fight against himself by fighting his wife. Satan and his cohorts who are the real enemies are usually left alone. In severe cases, the very existence of the real enemies is denied.

From other writings of Paul, we learn that the devil can take advantage of an ignorant person. This is what is written in 2 Corinthians 2:11: *"Lest satan should get an advantage of us: for we are not ignorant of his devices"* (King James Version). In order for satan to outwit you, you have to be ignorant of his strategies. Unfortunately, this describes a whole lot of people. Many men are uninformed of how the devil operates. They don't know that the devil is effectively using them to oppose the plan of God. It is because of the presence of this ignorance and darkness that the devil succeeds in the lives of many men. The devil thrives whenever he can operate in hiding.

Satan will do all that is in his power to keep you from ever knowing that marriage is a spiritual battle. He knows that if you ever know this powerful truth, you might be inclined to fight and try to break loose from his prison of darkness and ignorance.

Once you get to know that marriage is spiritual, you quickly realize the need to properly align yourself spiritually in order for your marriage to work at its optimum level. When you are properly aligned spiritually, you will understand that you are not supposed to war against flesh and blood. Your eyes are opened, and you see that your wife is not your enemy. It becomes clear that you are not supposed to use your ammunition against her.

If you do not align yourself properly in the spirit, you will keep wrestling against flesh and blood. You will keep thinking that your wife is not cute enough or smart enough, understanding enough or even spiritual enough! Consequently, you start building up other women who you perceive to be potentially cuter, smarter, more understanding, or more spiritual. Meanwhile, your wife will begin to fight against the other women (even when she does not know them), thereby creating a tense situation for you. When this happens, you are not able to fully benefit from any of the multiple relationships. It becomes a vicious cycle. The only being that will enjoy satisfaction is the devil.

Marriage was designed to be a daily reminder of the relationship between Christ and His church. Your own marriage can and should match this design. In order for this to happen, you have to first properly align yourself in the realm of the spirit.

The starting place in the process of spiritual alignment is submitting to the Father of spirits. He is the Architect of life and the Manufacturer of marriage. You submit to Him by asking Jesus Christ to become the Lord of your life. This means that you allow Jesus Christ to be the Boss of your life. You acknowledge that you belong to God and not to yourself or anyone else. You also acknowledge that your culture should not be the final authority in your life. You submit to God's Word as your final authority. You do what God says for you to do. You do not do what He forbids you to do.

How about putting this into practice and surrendering your life to Jesus Christ right now? Just take a moment to pray like this: "Father, I thank you for giving me this opportunity to properly connect with You. This moment I willingly surrender my life to You. Become the Lord of my life. Please, forgive me of all my sins. Permanently damage my ignorance. Wash me clean in the blood of Jesus. Restore me to the man you designed me to be. Make me an agent of change forever. Thank you for receiving me. I pray this in the name of Jesus—Amen!"

If you wholeheartedly prayed this prayer, I congratulate you for taking this bold step to initiate the process of spiritual alignment in your life. You are not going to be the same ever again! If you may please, take a moment to write me and let me know of your decision. I would be grateful. My contact information is provided at the end of this book.

If you are a married man, you will do well to take time out to ask your wife for her forgiveness for making her a victim of your ignorance. Inform her that you have found a new way of living! From now on, when she starts to observe positive changes in how you treat her, she will know that it is calculated and that it is not just a fleeting emotion.

Now that you know the truth about marriage, you are free to enjoy it and benefit fully from it. Marriage belongs to the realm of the spirit. It does not belong to the realms of the physical or the emotional. Without the spiritual component, all the other pieces will not properly hold together.

In the next chapters, we are going to discuss how to effectively live in the realm of the spirit.

Food For Thought

1. Lack of desire to know the truth carries repercussions.

2. Marriage is supposed to be a daily reminder of the destiny of the universal church—the bride of Christ.

3. A marriage is not about a husband and a wife.

4. Today can be the beginning of the rest of your life.

5. You cannot fully enjoy and benefit from a product if you do not know what it is and why it is.

Chapter 8

Functioning In Man's Real World

Quitters never win and winners never quit.
—Napoleon Hill

We established in the previous chapter that marriage belongs to the realm of the spirit. As people we have exposure to several different realms, kingdoms, or spheres. These different territories operate on different principles. Some laws that are valid in the earthly realm may not be applicable in the marine kingdom. Some rules that are legitimate in the plant kingdom may not be relevant in the animal kingdom.

From the biblical account of the creation of man, we learn that man is a spirit-being who resides in a physical body. As such, man belongs to the realm of the spirit because his essence is spirit. Now the realm of the spirit has its own set of principles and processes that are different from the laws of other kingdoms.

It is a cardinal principle in the realm of the spirit that for any man to transact any kind of business in that realm, that man has to have spiritual currency. This currency is called faith. It is the legal tender in the spirit kingdom. The author of the book of

Hebrews conclusively declares that *"it is impossible to please God without faith"* (Hebrews 11:6). In order for any man to effectively build a marriage relationship as we have discussed this far, that man has to have faith. This is because both man and marriage belong to the realm of the spirit. Faith is also a spirit. It is the exact opposite of faintheartedness.

> ### *Faith is the official currency in the spirit realm.*

From the writings of Paul, we learn that the process of exercising faith is not a passive one. To the contrary, it is a strenuous struggle. A man has to contend like an Olympian in order to apply this precious substance to life situations. In 1 Timothy 6:12, Paul instructs Timothy to *"fight the good fight of faith ..."* The Apostle Jude writes to exhort the believer to *"contend for the faith"* (Jude 1:3). Elsewhere in the Gospels it is clear that those who succeed in operating in the kingdom of God have to be forceful in their predisposition. Unfortunately, most men are deficient in courage. They easily succumb to fate.

The great marriage that you desire and dream about is a possibility. Unfortunately, no one is going to hand it to you on a platter. You will have to fight for it. And it is a fight to the finish. It is a winner-take-all type of battle.

Allow me to demonstrate from the Bible how to transact by faith in man's real world—the spirit world. Consider with me a story that is recorded in the book of 2 Kings 6:1–7. This is what is written there:

¹ One day the group of prophets came to Elisha and told him, "As you can see, this place where we meet with you is too small.
² Let's go down to the Jordan River, where there are plenty of logs. There we can build a new place for us to meet."
"All right," he told them, "go ahead."
³ "Please come with us," someone suggested.
"I will," he said.
⁴ So he went with them. When they arrived at the Jordan, they began cutting down trees.
⁵ But as one of them was cutting a tree, his ax head fell into the river. "Oh, sir!" he cried. "It was a borrowed ax!"
⁶ "Where did it fall?" the man of God asked. When he showed him the place, Elisha cut a stick and threw it into the water at that spot. Then the ax head floated to the surface.
⁷ "Grab it," Elisha said. And the man reached out and grabbed it.

According to the laws of the realm of science, this man's story should have ended when his ax head fell into the river. The laws of that realm do not allow for an ax head to float on water. The finance kingdom would definitely place this man in a poor credit-score category after he had lost a valuable borrowed item. Philanthropic logic would likely conclude that the best course of action is to have a community fund-raiser to help this man replace the lost ax head.

I am aware that when laws from other realms are applied to some marriages, those marriages appear hopeless. I am also fully aware that the Designer of marriage is on record saying there is nothing too hard for Him. As such, I choose to believe that when man applies the right principles to whatever situation, that situation will change for good.

Faith ignores the scientific laws, the financial principles, the logical conclusions, and the physical rules! It does not heed the experts' opinions. Faith sets aside all other regulations and engages the supernatural.

> ## *Faith refuses to yield to appearances.*

Take note that the man in the above story is unnamed. The man can be you or me.

The man knew that the group had not haphazardly gone to the Jordan. He was aware that they had made it their business to invite the man of God to go with them—for a reason. He understood that their relocation to the Jordan was not just a geographical move but a spiritually significant one. The man of God was like an official in the realm of the spirit. That is why when the man's ax head fell into the river, the man directed his cry to the man of God.

It is extremely important that you understand that when the ax head fell into the river, it did not cease to exist. It was there—only buried under a large volume of water. By virtue of its heaviness, the ax head must have gone straight to the bottom of the Jordan. Faith refuses to think of buying another ax head when there is one just sitting at the bottom of the river!

When a marriage relationship goes bad, it does not mean that the potential for that marriage to work out has vanished. It simply means there is room to exercise faith to turn that marriage around. Faith refuses to yield to appearances.

There are very high chances that the man had borrowed an ax because he could not afford to purchase one for himself. If he could not afford to buy one for himself, surely he could not afford to buy one for someone else. In the natural realm, he probably would have been forced to file for bankruptcy protection!

Thanks be to God, this man knew how to function in the realm of the spirit. The man was not a wimp. He was a fighter. He was not one to succumb to fate. He was not one to be forced to accept irrelevant laws of a different realm. In my spirit I can hear this man say to the river, "You may have swallowed up a lot of other objects before, but this is one ax head you will have to vomit somehow!" The river heard this man because in the realm of the spirit, everything has ears. Your marriage has ears. You need to speak to it.

> ### *In the realm of the spirit, everything has ears.*

I would be remiss to sound like I am minimizing this man's problem. To the contrary, I acknowledge that this brother was in very serious trouble. Losing valuable property belonging to someone else and not being able to replace it is a big deal.

From time to time, I encounter men who are overwhelmed by the magnitude of their problems. Some are overwhelmed to the extent of wanting to simply walk away from it all. Others are driven to the point of taking their lives. In the meantime, there are some would-be counselors who will advise these overwhelmed men not to surrender.

Should you happen to be in that place where your problems have converted themselves into giants and are trying to choke the life out of you, and everywhere you turn you are seeing nothing but problems, I want to counsel you to surrender! Just don't surrender to the problems or to fate. I advise you to learn from the example of the man in our story. You don't have to run out of town. You don't have to lose your mind. You don't have to die. Cry out and totally surrender to God. He has never failed, and He has never lost a battle. God is not going to start failing in your own case. The bigger the giants, the harder they will fall.

Faith also requires the willingness and ability to do some things that appear unintelligent and foolish. Cutting down a stick and throwing it in the river where the ax head fell does not look like much of a solution—to the natural mind that is. However, in the realm of the spirit, it proved to be the panacea in this man's situation.

> *Faith requires the willingness and ability to do some things that appear unintelligent and foolish.*

There are many men who simply need to acknowledge that they personally lost something as they were trying to build. Allow me to give some credit to the brother in our story. He was trying to do something good. He did not set out to lose someone else's ax head. He was trying to build. It just could be that he did not have the expertise in using an ax. It could be that the ax already had a problem and this brother did not know any better. It could even be that the tree he was cutting was too hard. Whatever the case, the brother was willing to take full responsibility for losing the ax head.

Not only was this man trying to do something that was good, he also had the humility to cry out for help when he needed help. This man had other possible options available to him. He could act all macho as if everything was okay. He could fake it and put up a show and continue swinging the handle in his hands as if he were still cutting the tree. Oh, that many men would quit playing games and be humble enough to cry out for help!

Help only came to the man because the man was able to take full responsibility for his actions. Also, help came after the man correctly identified the exact spot where he had lost the cutting edge! The man did not waste time beating about the bush and blaming the owner of the ax or the tree that he was cutting. He did not waste time threatening to file a lawsuit against the manufacturer of the ax. Many husbands can be helped if only they stop playing the blame game. Many husbands need to acknowledge that they blew it and lost the cutting edge of their marriages—especially in the area of building up their wives. It is only then that their marriages can recover the cutting edge.

> ### *You can recover the cutting edge in your life.*

The man in our story was a man who knew how to apply faith to his situation. When the ax head fell into the Jordan River, the man did not fold his hands and surrender his dream to fate.

You have to bear in mind that this man was pursuing a dream of expansion. That is why they had moved to the Jordan River in the first place. Then the devil decided to cripple this man's dream and make a mockery of the man's future.

Yes, in the natural, accidents do happen. However, this man was able to see beyond an apparent natural accident. Faith causes you to see beyond the circumstances surrounding you. Faith goes beyond the superficial, to the spirit behind a problem. It goes beyond the symptoms and deals with the root of the cause.

By faith, the man was able to realize that the devil was trying to cripple his dream. The ax head was pivotal to this man's attainment of his dream to expand and build a larger meeting place. This was not just about losing a valuable piece of iron—it was about a dream being snatched away. The man refused to give up on his vision. Instead, he chose to believe in what others call impossible.

There are many men the world over who have been cowed into abandoning their marriage-building projects. The devil snatched their wives and their dreams from them, and they accepted it. The devil offered them a destiny with alterations, and they sheepishly received it. They failed to realize that it was not about "just" losing a spouse. They did not comprehend that their losing of a spouse was much bigger than it appeared. It was about the devil meddling with God's eternal plan for humanity.

May I challenge you to determine to recover as much as you can of what was stolen from you? Determine to get back what you have lost. Like the man in our story, you can reach out and grab what the devil thought to have stolen from you. The word of the Lord to you is "grab it!" It is possible for you to recover your cutting edge. Cause the devil to regret that he ever stole from you. In keeping with the Word of God, cause him to pay you back seven times what he stole!

> ### *Disallow the devil to display your life as a trophy in hell.*

Finally, it is important to note that the man in our story had the ability to obey instructions. When the man of God instructed him to grab the ax head, the man obeyed without asking any questions. He had sense enough to know that he—not the man of God—needed the miracle. It is my sincere prayer that you be able to recognize what you need and do something about it. It is not an accident that you are reading this book right now. God knows that your miracle is within your reach. So—grab it!

Food For Thought

1. You are a spirit, you have a soul, and you live in a body.

2. Every realm has its own laws.

3. There is nothing too hard for God. He has never failed. He has never lost a battle. He can handle your case.

4. Many husbands can be helped if only they stop playing the blame game.

5. There is no tenable excuse for you to fail.

Chapter 9

The Portrait Of A Great Man

It is possible for the man to evolve to look like his portrait.
—T. Munyaradzi

The opposite of a fainthearted man is a courageous man. A courageous man makes for a great man. I am quite sure that it would be an interesting project to solicit people's opinions and descriptions of what a "great man" looks like. More interesting would be the varying strengths of conviction behind the opinions.

There certainly would be those who present their opinions simply as that—their opinions. On the other hand, there would be those who present their opinions as if they were the whole truth and the only truth. Somewhere in between would also be a good number of others.

Most interesting would be the observation of the varying degrees of openness to learning of those who share their opinions. Those who hold loosely to their opinions would likely be more open to learning. Those who are satisfied with their opinions would likely be further ahead on the path to perpetual ignorance.

Placing the list of people's opinions in juxtaposition to God's list of the characteristics of a great man would expose a vast difference in perception between God and man.

In a sense, this chapter lets us take a look at God's portrait of a great man. In fact, Jesus went as far as saying that this particular man was greater than all the men who had ever lived up to his time. Wow! What a compliment from the mouth of God!

> ### *Those who are not open to learning are further ahead on the path to perpetual ignorance.*

The name of the man in question is John. Many people know him as John the Baptist. This is the man who was Jesus's forerunner. We learn from the Gospel writers that at some point in time, John was arrested and put into prison. After he had been languishing in prison for a good while, John sent some of his disciples to Jesus with a piercing question. Here is the question that John sent to Jesus in Matthew 11:3: *"Are you the Messiah we've been expecting, or should we keep looking for someone else?"*

It is kind of confusing for John to ask such a question. A study of the Gospels reveals that this John, who was born miraculously, came to earth for one reason. That reason was to prepare the way for Jesus the Christ. It was John who made a bold and confident introduction of Jesus to the nation of Israel. It is written in John 1:29–30: *"The next day John saw Jesus coming toward him and said, 'Look! The Lamb of God who takes away the sin of the world! He is the One I was talking about when I said, "A man is coming after me who is far greater than I am, for He existed long before me."'"*

As such, John's question to Jesus could be interpreted as a vote of no confidence. It is generally believed that John asked this question because he expected that Jesus would do something to get him out of prison, but Jesus did not. It is very amazing what men can say or do when other men do not live up to their high expectations of them.

Jesus did not retaliate to John's no-confidence motion. In actuality, Jesus did not directly answer John's query. Jesus simply instructed John's disciples to *"go back to John and tell him what you have heard and seen—the blind see, the lame walk, the lepers are cured, the deaf hear, the dead are raised to life, and the Good News is being preached to the poor"* (Matthew 11:4–5). Supposedly, this would help John to decipher for himself if Jesus was the real Messiah or not.

It was right after this event that Jesus picked up a verbal "paintbrush" and started painting His "portrait of a great man." The description is found in the Gospel according to Matthew 11:7–11:

> *[7]As John's disciples were leaving, Jesus began talking about him to the crowds. "What kind of man did you go into the wilderness to see? Was he a weak reed, swayed by every breath of wind?"*

Obviously, Jesus's crowd knew what a reed was and what it meant for a man to be likened to a reed.

A reed is a tall, slim plant that grows near water. Because of the reed's physical structure, it happens that the reed bends in whichever direction the wind blows. If the wind blows toward the south, the reed bends over toward the south. If the wind blows toward the north, the reed leans toward the north. If the wind blows east or west, that is the direction toward which the reed leans. The direction of the reed is as changeable as the wind. A weak reed, swayed by every breath of wind, is a symbol of instability.

Before John was incarcerated, crowds of people used to go and listen to him preaching in the wilderness. Even King Herod had gone down a few times to hear John preach.

During His "portrait-painting session," Jesus used three sets of rhetorical questions to tell the crowds what He thought about John. The first set of questions was this: *"What kind of man did you go into the wilderness to see? Was he a weak reed, swayed by every breath of wind?"*

In a picturesque way, Jesus was telling the crowds that John was not an unstable, wishy-washy, yellow-belly type of a man. John was not an indecisive man. He was not a spineless man. A weak reed swayed by every breath of wind is figurative of inconsistency, unpredictability, and cowardice. It is a representation of a wavering man. It is a picture of a man who readily yields to all forces—great or small—that come against him. It also suggests a man who is uneasy.

It is very difficult to have meaningful dealings with a weak-reed-swayed-by-every-breath-of-wind type of a man. This is because such a man is not dependable. He is the kind of man who is constantly changing his mind. Consequently, that man's word is meaningless because he will soon forget whatever he said and change on to something else. As such, you cannot trust that kind of a man.

A weak-reed-swayed-by-every-breath-of-wind type of a man is a man who won't lead. The key word here is won't. It is not that he can't—he just won't. This is because he cannot stand up for anything. The reason he cannot stand up for anything is because he has no backbone.

There was one such man in the Bible. This man was naturally positioned for leadership, but he had to be disqualified from the task. This man was named Reuben. He was Jacob's firstborn son. Jacob, whose name was later changed to Israel, was the founder of the nation of Israel. So Reuben was the natural heir apparent to his father, Israel. A part of Reuben's story is told in the book of Genesis 49:1–4.

> ¹*And Jacob called unto his sons, and said, Gather yourselves together, that I may tell you that which shall befall you in the last days.*
> ²*Gather yourselves together, and hear, ye sons of Jacob; and hearken unto Israel your father.*
> ³*Reuben, thou art my firstborn, my might, and the beginning of my strength, the excellency of dignity, and the excellency of power:*
> ⁴*Unstable as water, thou shalt not excel; because thou wentest up to thy father's bed; then defiledst thou it: he went up to my couch.* (King James Version)

Jacob said of his firstborn son Reuben that he was "*unstable as water.*" In what way is water unstable you may ask? Water is known to be a very important substance. Its physical and chemical properties make it unique. The most well-known physical properties of water are that it is colorless, it is tasteless, and it is odorless. Because it is colorless, water will take the color of whatever it is mixed with. Because it is tasteless, water will taste like whatever substance it is blended with. By the same token, water will smell like whatever substance it is mixed with.

It turns out that a man who is unstable as water has no character. If you put him with holy brothers, he will be a holy man. If you put him with a different crowd, he will be like that crowd. On his own he cannot stand up for anything. He has a very poor sense of right and wrong. Because of that, if a chance to sleep with his father's wife ever presents itself—he will jump on it! No big deal because he is unstable as water.

Jesus clearly paints the picture of John as a man who was not like a weak reed swayed by every breath of wind. To the contrary, John was a very stable man. He was more like an oak tree that stood solid and straight. John was not the kind of man who could be flattered by popularity. Rejection did not bother him either. John knew who he was and what he was about. He was a firm and resolute man. Jesus's crowd knew John to be that kind of a man.

Many men become like a weak reed swayed by every breath of wind because they lack convictions. The dictionary meaning of conviction is "a fixed or firm belief." Convictions are supposed to deal with things that a person has become fully convinced of, having been persuaded by evidence or argument. They are supposed to be founded upon facts and thorough investigation.

It happens that a man's convictions, or lack thereof, determine his character, which in turn influences his conduct. What a man believes determines who he becomes and influences how he behaves. In a Christian context, convictions have to do with how a man takes the teachings of the Word of God and applies them to his life on a daily basis. Without controversy, a Christian man's convictions should be based on the word of God.

I want you to think for a moment about people who have had a lasting impact on your life. They probably are or were people with strong convictions. There is a correlation between the strength of a person's convictions and the amount of impact the person has on other people. It turns out that the stronger the convictions, the greater the impact.

> ## *Many men lack convictions.*

When a man is lazy to develop convictions, he will drift along with different ever-changing currents of life. He becomes like a weak reed, swayed by every breath of wind.

Jesus continued his painting by asking the crowds a second set of abstract questions found in Matthew 11:8. It is written, *"But what went ye out for to see? A man clothed in soft raiment? Behold, they that wear soft clothing are in kings' houses"* (King James Version).

It is important to bear in mind that Jesus did not speak in the English language! Mainly, Jesus spoke in either Aramaic or Greek. Most of the New Testament was originally written in the Greek language. The Greek word that was translated into the English as *soft* in Matthew 11:8 is the word *malakos*. In its etymological form, malakos means soft to the touch. In its metaphorical form, it means an effeminate man.

This time around Jesus was highlighting the fact that John was not a delicate and flimsy man. John was not a softie! This is a depiction of a man who tries to look like and or behave like a woman. The problem with this kind of a man is that he is not convincing. Something about him is questionable. He lacks credibility. There is something about this kind of a man that tells onlookers that you cannot trust him.

John was the exact opposite of a man clothed in soft raiment, literally and metaphorically. Again, Matthew, the Gospel writer, tells us that *"John's clothes were woven from coarse camel hair, and he wore a leather belt around his waist ..."* (Matthew 3:4). John was a convincing guy. There was toughness about him. He preached in the wilderness, and people came from the towns and cities to hear him. Not because he sent out flyers or aired some TV commercials! John did not even have a microphone. He was the kind of man that people could follow.

As He was making His final touches of the portrait, Jesus asked yet another set of questions, and then He made His final remarks.

> *⁹But what went ye out for to see? A prophet? Yea, I say unto you, and more than a prophet.*
> *¹⁰For this is he, of whom it is written, Behold, I send my messenger before thy face, which shall prepare thy way before thee.*
> *¹¹Verily I say unto you, among them that are born of women there hath not risen a greater than John the Baptist: notwithstanding he that is least in the kingdom of heaven is greater than he.* (Matthew 11)

Jesus concludes by telling His crowd categorically that the man that they went out to see in the wilderness was a great man. Jesus calls John a prophet. A prophet is a man who is moved by the Spirit of God. This gave John and a weak reed swayed by every breath something in common. They are both swayable material. The only difference is what sways them. According to Jesus, a man is only great to the extent that he can yield to the Spirit of God and stand against other forces.

> ### *A man is only great to the extent that he can yield to the Spirit of God.*

Some men do not yield to the Spirit of God at all. Others yield to a limited extent. Then there are others who completely surrender to the Spirit of God. The differences in the amount of yielding to God constitute different levels of greatness. Of course there are men who are not great at all! Some men are great. Others are very great. There are others who are exceedingly great.

The best news that Jesus gave to His crowd was that any one of them could potentially be greater than John. John came preaching about the kingdom of God, but he himself was not in it. Jesus had not yet offered His life for mankind to give mankind access into the kingdom of God. When a man enters into the kingdom of God by fully submitting to the kingship of Jesus Christ, that man is greater than John.

It is very interesting to note that Jesus said the very best about John after John said the worst about Jesus. May I conclude by saying the best about you? Wherever you are in your personal growth process, you can evolve to look like the picture of you that God has. Your portrait in God's custody depicts a man who is not a coward. It is a picture of a man who can embrace truth and appropriate it in his daily life. It is the most beautiful picture of a man, who after reading this, is not going back to the chains of ignorance and the prison of denial. It is a picture of you.

Food For Thought

1. What is your description of a great man?

2. What would you do if your opinion about a product is different from the opinion of the manufacturer of the product?

3. Your task is not to seek to be a great man but to identify and remove all the barriers within you that you have consciously or unconsciously built against greatness.

4. Be committed to your convictions but stay open to learning.

5. Your present address does not have to be your final address.

NOTES

If you want to know more about Not for the Fainthearted seminars, or if you want to communicate with the author for any reason, send correspondence to the following e-mail or regular mail address:

04thefainthearted@sbcglobal.net
or
2424 Poinciana Place
Dallas, Texas 75212
U.S.A.